UNIVERSITY PRESS

Great Clarendon Street, Oxford OX2 6DP

Oxford University Press is a department of the University of Oxford.
It furthers the University's objective of excellence in research, scholarship,
and education by publishing worldwide in

Oxford   New York

Auckland Cape Town Dar es Salaam Hong Kong Karachi
Kuala Lumpur Madrid Melbourne Mexico City Nairobi
New Delhi Shanghai Taipei Toronto

With offices in

Argentina Austria Brazil Chile Czech Republic France Greece
Guatemala Hungary Italy Japan Poland Portugal Singapore
South Korea Switzerland Thailand Turkey Ukraine Vietnam

with associated companies in Berlin Ibadan
Oxford is a registered trade mark of Oxford University Press
in the UK and in certain other countries

British Library Cataloguing in Publication Data available

ISBN 978-0-19-273183-8 (paperback)

1 3 5 7 9 10 8 6 4 2

Printed in China

Paper used in the production of this book is a natural, recyclable product made
from wood grown in sustainable forests. The manufacturing process conforms
to the environmental regulations of the country of origin

See You Later, Escalator

Escalator

Rhymes for the very young

Compiled by **John Foster**

OXFORD
UNIVERSITY PRESS

Contents

See You Later, Escalator

See you later, escalator!
In a blink, fizzy drink.

See you later, rollerskater!
In a tick, lolly stick.

See you later, mashed potata!
In an hour, cauliflower.

See you later, escalator!
In a smile, crocodile.

John Foster

When All The Cows Were Sleeping

When all the cows were sleeping
And the sun had gone to bed
Up jumped the scarecrow
And this is what he said
I'm a dingle, dangle scarecrow
With a flippy, floppy hat
I can shake my hands like this
And shake my feet like that
When all the hens were roosting
And the moon behind the cloud
Up jumped the scarecrow
And shouted very loud . . .

M. Russell Smith and G. Russell Smith

10

Knick Knack

Knick Knack Paddywhack
Rolling stone.
I saw a dog with a mobile phone.
He was wag, wag, wagging
His long, black tail,
So I knew right then
That he had some mail.
Knick Knack Paddywhack
Rolling stone.
I saw a dog with a mobile phone.

John Kitching

11

Katy Kelly

Katy Kelly
watched the telly
lying in a dish of jelly.
Though smooth and soft
beneath her belly,
watching telly
in a jelly,
soon made
Katy Kelly
smelly!

Brenda Williams

12

Lively Lou and Lazy Lynn

Lively Lou and Lazy Lynn
One went out and the other stayed in
One got up and the other sat down
One gave a smile and the other gave a frown
One made her bed and the other made a mess
One wore jeans and the other wore a dress.
One liked jam and one liked cheese
Lazy Lynn and her twin Louise.

Trevor Millum

Jilliky Jolliky Jelliky Jee

Jilliky Jolliky Jelliky Jee,
three little cooks in a coconut tree
one cooked a peanut and one cooked a pea,
one brewed a thimble of cinnamon tea,
then they sat down to a dinner for three,
Jilliky Jolliky Jelliky Jee.

Jack Prelutsky

Mary Anne

Little Mary Anne
was really quite fantastic.
She wasn't like her friends
cos she was made of elastic.

She'd roll herself up
to become very small,
then jump up and down
and bounce like a ball.

One day a man came
to measure Mary Anne
from foot to head
and from hand to hand.

With no further ado
the girl was fetched
and with a smile on her face
she stretched and stretched.

She stretched and stretched
this amazing girl
she stretched and stretched
right round the world.

This made her so hot
she began to smoke.
There was a sudden snap
and she suddenly broke.

It was a terrible shame
that it was all so drastic
but that's what happens
if you're made of elastic.

Michael Rosen

She'd tie her leg to the gate
and make her other leg hop,
the elastic would stretch
and take her to the shop.

She could leave a room
and you wouldn't mind
but then you'd discover
she'd left her eyes behind.

She might be upstairs
eating jelly;
while you're downstairs
she'd tickle your belly.

She could tie her hand to the table
(this was a wicked trick)
stretch out and let go
and give you a terrible flick.

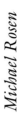

Humpty Dumpty

Humpty Dumpty
Sat on a wall,
To watch
A football match;
He shouted and cheered
Till he tumbled off,
And fell in
A strawberry patch!

John Cunliffe

One Man Went to Mow

One man went to mow,
He couldn't work the mower,
He used a pair of scissors, so
The grass got cut much slower.

Kaye Umansky

16

Yankee Doodle

Yankee Doodle came to town,
Did he take a bus?
No, he put a saddle
On a hippopotamus.

Richard Edwards

Hide and Sheep

We're Bo Peep's sheep,
But shhh! Don't tell,
We're hiding down
The Ding Dong Well.

We're Bo Peep's sheep,
She'll never find us
If we keep our
Tails behind us.

We're Bo Peep's sheep,
We'll count to ten,
Then sneak and creep
Back home again.

We're Bo Peep's sheep,
We may look tame,
But BOO!! It's us . . .
We've won the game.

Clare Bevan

Jack and the Yak

There was a young fellow called Jack
Who went for a ride on a Yak
   When he gave it a smack
   It raced off down the track
And came back without Jack on its back.

John Foster

Up and Down the City Road

Up and down the city road,
Round and round the market,
Riding on my dinosaur,
Wherever can I park it?

Richard Edwards

yum
yum

The Dinosaur's Dinner

Once a mighty dinosaur
Came to dine with me,
He gobbled up the curtains
And swallowed our settee.

He didn't seem to fancy
Onion soup with crusty bread,
He much preferred the flavour
Of our furniture instead.

He ate up all our dining-chairs
And carpets from the floor,
He polished off the table, then
He looked around for more.

The television disappeared
In one almighty gulp,
Wardrobes, beds, and bathroom
He crunched into a pulp.

He really loved the greenhouse,
He liked the garden shed,
He started on the chimney-pots
But then my mother said:

'Your friends are always welcome
To drop in for a bite,
But really this one seems to have
A giant appetite.

You'd better take him somewhere else,
I'm sure I don't know where,
I only know this friend of yours
Needs more than we can spare!'

And suddenly I realized
I knew the very place,
And when I showed him where it was
You should have seen his face—

I don't think I've seen anyone
Enjoy a dinner more,
I watched him wander on his way,
A happy dinosaur!

The council did rebuild our school,
But that of course took time . . .
And all because a dinosaur
Came home with me to dine!

June Crebbin

Big is Beautiful!!

The Dragon's Birthday Party

It's the dragon's birthday party,
he's ten years old today.
'Come and do your special trick,'
I heard his mother say.

We crowded round the table,
we pushed and shoved to see,
as someone brought the cake mix in;
the dragon laughed with glee.

It was just a bowl with flour in
and eggs and milk and that
with ten blue candles round the top
in the shape of Postman Pat.

The dragon took a big deep breath
stood up to his full size
and blew a blast of smoke and flame
that made us shut our eyes.

We felt the air grow hotter
we knew the taste of fear.
I felt a spark fly through the air
and land on my left ear.

But when we looked,
make no mistake:
the candles were lit
and the cake was baked.

Ian McMillan

Here Come the Creatures

Here come the Creatures,
  One!
  Two!
  Three!
A crocodile's holding hands with a flea.
A zebra's arm-in-arm with a bee.
A tiger's toddling on with a rat.
An emu's knocking about with a bat.
A warthog's dancing along with a wren.
An elephant's side by side with a hen.
Here come the Creatures,
  Eight!
  Nine!
  Ten!

Wes Magee

Our Dog

Our dog chases kids on skates,
   He does it every day,
And if he doesn't stop it soon,
   I'll take his skates away.

Aislinn and Larry O'Loughlin

The Hamster's Wheel

Hamster, running round your wheel,
You're keeping very busy.
Hamster, tell me how you feel?
I'm feeling very dizzy!

Gordon Snell

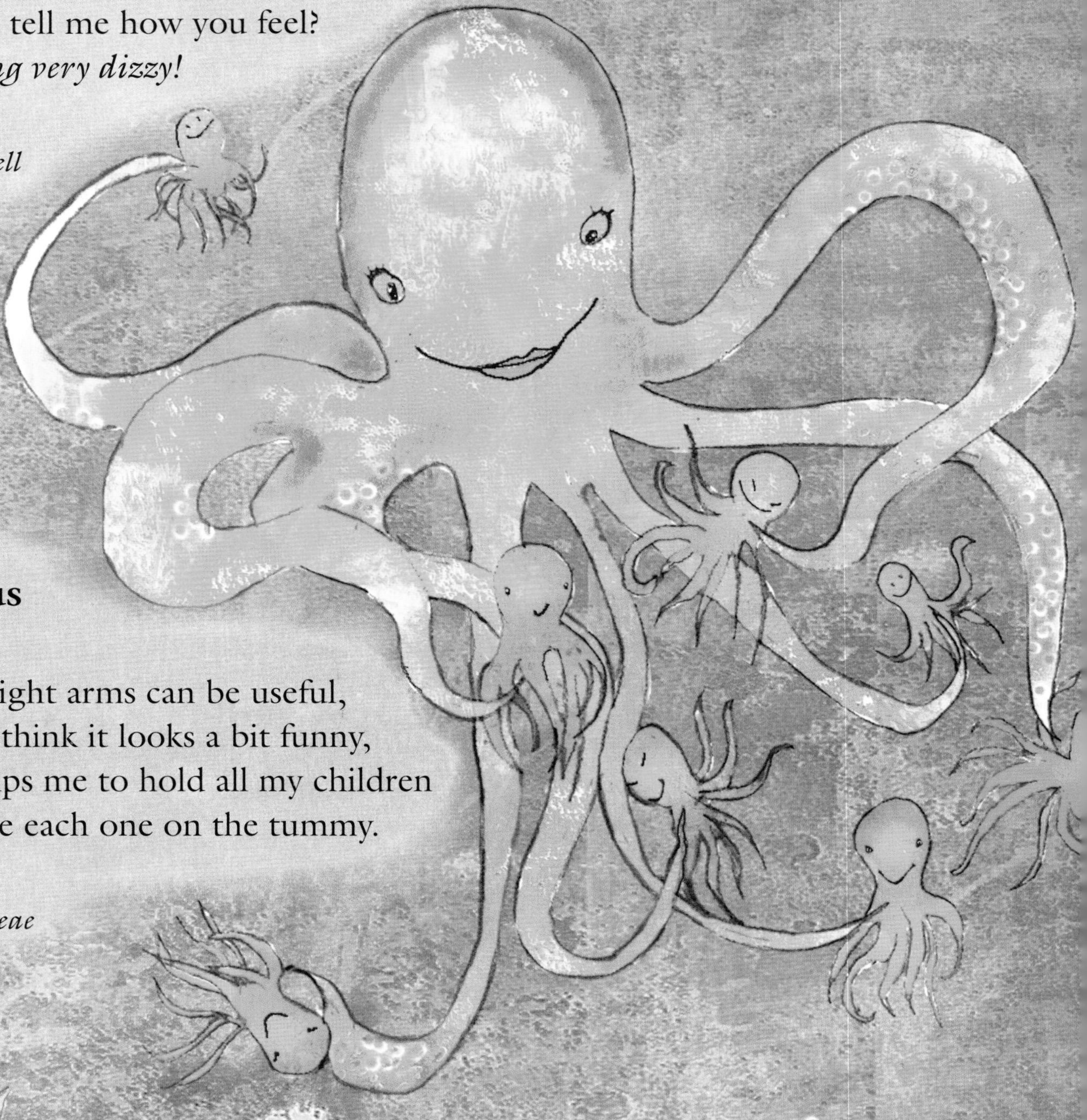

Octopus

Having eight arms can be useful,
You may think it looks a bit funny,
But it helps me to hold all my children
And tickle each one on the tummy.

Giles Andreae

Bored

Brian the lion,
Samantha the panther,
And Rita the cheetah
Were horribly bored.
So they stood on a hill
In deepest Brazil
And they roared and they roared
And they roared and they
ROARED!

'Enough of this roaring,'
Said Brian the lion,
'My throat's really sore
And it's hurting my head.
I want to be quiet.
I think we should try it.'
And so they went home
And played Twister™ instead.

Kaye Umansky

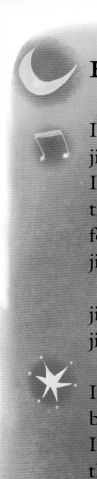
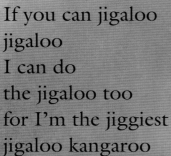

Hopaloo Kangaroo

If you can jigaloo
jigaloo
I can do
the jigaloo too
for I'm the jiggiest
jigaloo kangaroo

jigaloo all night through
jigaloo all night through

If you can boogaloo
boogaloo
I can do
the boogaloo too
for I'm the boogiest
boogaloo kangaroo

boogaloo all night through
boogaloo all night through

But bet you can't hopaloo
hopaloo
like I can do
for I'm the hoppiest
hopaloo kangaroo

hopaloo all night through
hopaloo all night through

Gonna show you steps
you never knew.
And guess what, guys?
My baby in my pouch
will be dancing too.

John Agard

28

Gorilla!

I'm a Gorilla!
I'm a Gorilla!
I want ice cream
And I want vanilla!
Three big scoops
On a dish with a spoon.
I want ice cream
And I want it **SOON**.

Kaye Umansky

The Dancing Tiger

There's a quiet, gentle tiger
In the woods below the hill,
And he dances on his tiptoes,
When the world is dreaming still.
So you only ever hear him
In the silence of the night,
And you only ever see him
When the full moon's shining bright.

One summer night I saw him first—
Twirling, whirling round.
And when I gasped aloud in fright,
He knew that he'd been found.
He turned to me and whispered,
'Please don't tell them that I'm here.'
The laughter in his lightning eyes
Swept away my fear.
'If you will keep me secret—
Never tell a soul—
Then you can come and dance with me,
On nights the moon is whole.'

So once a month, from then till now,
I've tiptoed to the wood.
We've swirled and swayed among the trees,
As Tiger said we could.
We've skipped in spring through bluebells,
In summer circled slow,
We've high-kicked in the autumn leaves,
And waltzed in winter snow.

But now that I am eighty-two
My dancing nights are done.
I've chosen you, great-grandchild,
To share my dream, so come
With me into the woods of sleep—
The full moon's shining high—
I'll sit and watch you dancing both
Beneath the starbright sky.

Malachy Doyle

31

grOoOwll!

UhoOooot!

Hooooot!

There's Nothing

There's nothing quite as
yappy as a dog
There's nothing quite as
snappy as a shark
As curly as an eel
As chirpy as a lark
There's nothing quite as
YAPPY
   as
      a
         dog

There's nothing quite as
hooty as an owl
There's nothing quite as
snooty as a cat
As nippy as a fox
As zippy as a bat
There's nothing quite as
hooooooooty
   as
      an
         owl

Curly...

Hooow!!..

There's nothing quite as
cosy as a mouse
There's nothing quite as
holey as a mole
As wiffy as a skunk
As sniffy as a vole
There's nothing quite as
cosy
      as
          a
              mouse

There's nothing quite as
growly as a bear
There's nothing quite as
howly as a wolf
As flighty as a fish
As mighty as a bull
There's nothing quite as
G R O W L Y
      as
          a
              bear!

James Carter

If I Were a Hawk

If I were a hawk I'd circle and stalk,
If I were a toad I'd waddle and walk,
If I were a panther I'd prowl and I'd pace,
If I were a zebra I'd rear and I'd race,
If I were a seagull I'd soar and I'd sail,
If I were a slug I'd trudge and I'd trail,
If I were a snake I'd slide and I'd slither,
If I were a sloth I'd doze and I'd dither,
If I were a hippo I'd trundle and tramp,
If I were a rhino I'd stumble and stamp,
If I were a firefly I'd dart and I'd dance,
If I were a pony I'd plunge and I'd prance,
If I were a swordfish I'd spin and I'd spike—

But as I'm just me
        I'll ride on my bike.

Clare Bevan

My Roller Boots

When I put on my roller boots
I think it's quite a puzzle
That when those boots are on my feet
My legs get in a muddle.

For one leg goes this way,
And one leg goes that,
Then I wibble and I wobble
And . . . WHOOPS . . . I fall down flat!

Cynthia Rider

Finger Paints

Finger paints are
   cool as mud,
Mud that's red or blue.
They squish and squash
And slide most any
Way I want them to.

I can squeeze a bump of green
Or swish it up and down
Or make it stop
   right on top
Of a humpy hill of brown.

If someone says,
'Do tell us, dear,
What *does* your picture say?'
I swoosh the picture all around
And make it go away.

Lilian Moore

Waiting for Mum

Ink in my earhole
Clay up my nose
Dirt on my fingers
Mud on my clothes.

Bright green painting
Bright green hair
Brand new jacket
Brand new tear.

Waiting for Mum
To take me out to tea
Got a funny feeling
She won't be pleased with me.

Peter Dixon

Rosemary Rudd

Rosemary Rudd
Says, 'I like mud!'

It's squelchy! It's gooey!
It's sticky! It's gluey!

You can pick it up and hold it.
You can shape it. You can mould it.

It slips and it slops.
It drips and it drops.

It gets between your fingers.
It gets between your toes.
It gets itself all over you—
It gets right up your nose!

It gets in your ears.
It gets in your hair.
But Rosemary Rudd says,
'I don't care.'

Rosemary Rudd
Says, 'I like mud!'

John Foster

Weather

Dot a dot dot dot a dot dot
Spotting the window-pane.
Spack a spack speck flick a flack fleck
Freckling the window-pane.

A spatter a scatter a wet cat a clatter
A splatter a rumble outside.
Umbrella umbrella umbrella umbrella
Bumbershoot barrel of rain.

Slosh a galosh slosh a galosh
Slither and slather and glide
A puddle a jump a puddle a jump
A puddle a jump puddle splosh
A juddle a pump aluddle a dump a
Puddmuddle jump in and slide!

Eve Merriam

39

Marmaduke Monkey and Barnabas Bear

Marmaduke monkey and Barnabas bear
went out with no coats on to visit the fair.
With no hats or umbrellas, no jumpers, the pair
went, skipping quite happily off to the fair.

Though the weatherman said there would be a big storm
they refused to put anything on that was warm
and Marmaduke monkey and Barnabas bear
were soaked to their skins as they got to the fair
but they danced in the rain. They didn't care
as they bounced through the puddles and mud at the fair.

Marian Swinger

40

Storm

It's raining, it's raining, it's raining,
And leaves have stuck to my face.
The wind's snatched my hat—
I'm trying to catch it—
But the wind is winning the race.

Michelle Magorian

Skirts and Shirts and Dressing Gowns

Skirts and shirts and dressing gowns—
The wind begins to blow—
They're like a family upside down
Dancing in a row!

Laurence Anholt

41

Best of All

In autumn when
The leaves fall down,
I love the red,
The gold, the brown.

In winter time
I like the snow,
It's always sad
To see it go.

I like to see
The lambs in spring,
When birds in treetops
Start to sing.

But summer's best
Of all the lot,
When the sun shines down
And makes it hot.

Clive Webster

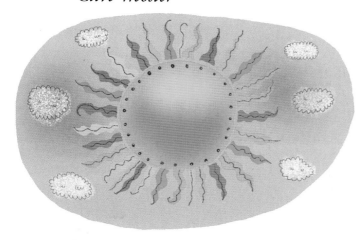

Summer Days

I'm looking for a hot spot.
A what spot?
A hot spot.
I'm looking for a hot spot
To lie out in the sun.
I'm looking for a hot spot
To play and have some fun.
I'm looking for a hot spot
To hit a ball and run.
Oh, I'm looking for a hot spot.
A what spot?
A hot spot.
I'm looking for a hot spot
Now summer has begun.

Anne English

A Summer Afternoon

High above the grass,
Swinging through the air,
Granny, me, and Smoky
In her garden chair.

Faces to the sun.
Noses lifted high,
Watching all the clouds
Come closer as we fly.

Michelle Magorian

Rolling Down a Hill

I'm rolling
rolling
rolling
down

I'm rolling
down a
hill.

I'm rolling
rolling
rolling
down

I'm rolling
down it
still.

44

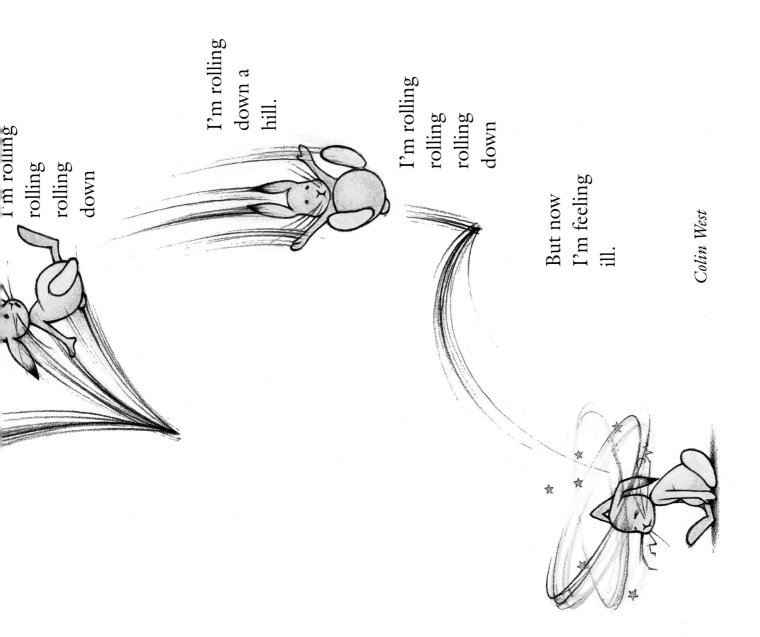

I'm rolling
rolling
rolling
down

I'm rolling
down a
hill.

I'm rolling
rolling
rolling
down

But now
I'm feeling
ill.

Colin West

45

Hey, Bug!

Hey, bug, stay!
Don't run away.
I know a game that we can play.

I'll hold my fingers very still
And you can climb a finger-hill.

No, no.
Don't go.

Here's a wall—a tower, too,
a tiny bug-town, just for you.
I've a cookie. You have some.
Take this oatmeal cookie crumb.

Hey, bug, stay!
Hey, bug!
Hey!

Lilian Moore

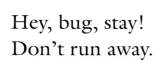

46

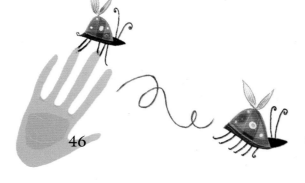

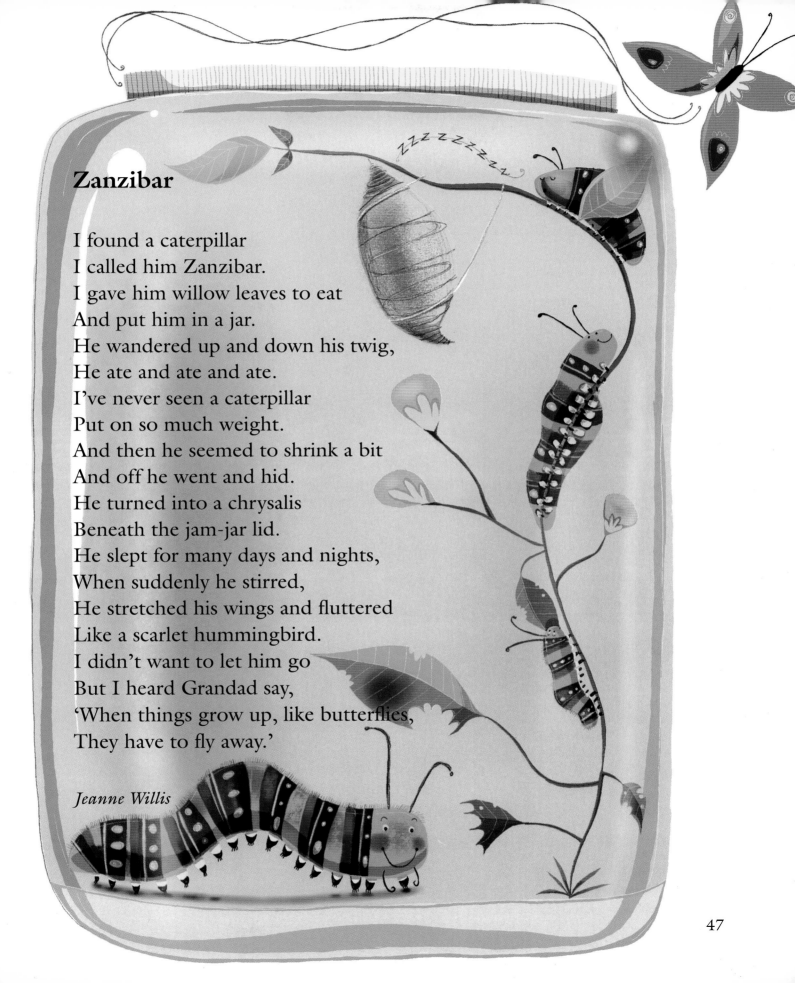

Zanzibar

I found a caterpillar
I called him Zanzibar.
I gave him willow leaves to eat
And put him in a jar.
He wandered up and down his twig,
He ate and ate and ate.
I've never seen a caterpillar
Put on so much weight.
And then he seemed to shrink a bit
And off he went and hid.
He turned into a chrysalis
Beneath the jam-jar lid.
He slept for many days and nights,
When suddenly he stirred,
He stretched his wings and fluttered
Like a scarlet hummingbird.
I didn't want to let him go
But I heard Grandad say,
'When things grow up, like butterflies,
They have to fly away.'

Jeanne Willis

The Wuzzy Wasps of Wasperton

The wuzzy wasps of Wasperton
Are buzzing round the plums
And sucking all the juicy ones
Before somebody comes.

The wuzzy wasps of Wasperton
Are buzzing round the pears
And choosing all the ripest ones—
They think the orchard's theirs.

The wuzzy wasps of Wasperton
Steal fruit fit for a king.
But don't disturb them if you go—
Those wuzzy wasps can STING!

Daphne Lister

48

Mumbling Bees

All around the garden flowers
Big velvet bees go bumbling,
They hover low and as they go
They're mumbling, mumbling, mumbling.

To lavender and snapdragons
The busy bees keep coming,
And all the busy afternoon
They're humming, humming, humming.

Inside each bell-shaped flower and rose
They busily go stumbling,
Collecting pollen all day long
And bumbling, bumbling, bumbling.

Daphne Lister

Picnic Tea

We found a shady spot under a tree.
Here's what we had for our picnic tea.

We had ants in the sandwiches
        wasps in the jam,
        slugs in the lettuce leaves,
        beetles in the ham,
        midges in the orange juice,
        flies on the cheese,
        spiders on the sausages,
        ice-cream full of bees!

David Harmer

Going Swimming

Kick off your shoes, pull off your clothes,
The pool smell tingles up your nose.

That shower is freezing—shiver, shout—
Leap in the water, splash about.

Doggy paddle, slip and slop,
Jump and dive and belly flop.

Splosh the breaststroke, plunge the crawl,
Float on your back, and throw a ball.

Before you know an hour's gone by—
Another shower—a brisk rub dry.

And then the best part of the treat—
A bag of fish and chips to eat.

Alison Chisholm

The Beach Boys

Other children
On the sand
Take a bucket
In each hand,
Build a castle
See it rise
Underneath the
Seagull skies.

Golden towers,
Seaweed flowers,
Salty moats
For feather boats,
Pebble walls
By waterfalls,
Shells and stones
And white, white bones
Mark the windows,
Line the floors,
Decorate the
Palace doors.

We just work like
Seaside moles
Digging lots of muddy
HOLES !!

Clare Bevan

52

The Sandcastle

We built a huge sandcastle
With turrets and with towers.
We decorated it with shells.
It took us hours and hours.

We left it standing on the beach,
And went to the park to play.
When we got back, the sea had come
And washed it all away.

John Foster

53

Up on Daddy's Shoulders

When Daddy sits me on his shoulders
I see far beyond the trees.
But when he puts me down again
All I see are knees!

There are dimply knees
And pimply knees
And knees as pink as jellies.
Knees under shorts,
Knees over socks
And grubby knees in wellies.

54

Then Daddy sits me on his shoulders
And I'm high above the town,
But I'm in amongst those knees again
When Daddy puts me down.

Skip-skitter knees,
Keep fitter knees
And knees content to laze.
I know everybody
By their knees
And no one by their face!

I suppose I'll see the whole wide world
When I'm a little older.
But I hope I'll never be too big
To sit on Daddy's shoulders.

Maureen Haselhurst

55

My Sister

My sister likes bananas
That's all she'll ever eat.
She even keeps the skins
And wears them on her feet.

My sister eats bananas
Breakfast, lunch, and tea
Then swings upon the curtains
Just like a chimpanzee.

John Coldwell

Ali's Dinner

When Ali eats his dinner
some goes in his mouth,
but peas and beans and leafy greens
fly east and west and south!

When Ali eats his pudding,
most of it ends on his vest;
some somehow crawls on to our walls
and some flies north and west!

Judith Nicholls

57

Gooseberry Juiceberry

Gooseberry,
Juiceberry,
Loose berry jam.

Spread it on crackers,
Spread it on bread,
Try not to spread it
On to your head.

Gooseberry,
Juiceberry,
Loose berry jam.

No matter how neatly
You try to bite in,
It runs like a river
Down to your chin.

Gooseberry,
Juiceberry,
Loose berry jam.

Eve Merriam

58

Sticky Syrup

Sweet and sticky syrup drops
from sticky syrup bottle tops.
Sticky table, sticky floor,
sticky syrup's hard to pour.

Sticky golden gleaming lakes
of sticky syrup on pancakes.
Sticky syrup, thick and sweet,
sticky syrup's good to eat.

Sticky lips and sticky fingers,
sweet and sticky syrup lingers,
trickling in golden streams . . .
Syrup's in my sweetest dreams.

Jane Clarke

59

Ready for Spaghetti

Pasta ribbons, pasta bows,
Pasta spirals, pasta O's,
Some is white and some is green,
Some comes with spinach in between.

It's shaped like tubes and wheels and strings
And named all sorts of funny things:
Ravioli, Tortellini,
Macaroni, and Linguini.

In my book it is supreme;
I like it best with peas and cream.
Pasta—there's no way to beat it.
The only thing to do is eat it!

Peggy Guthart

Food for the Week

Sausages on Mondays,
brown and sizzling hot.
    Curry's the dish for Tuesdays,
    all spicy from the pot.
Hamburgers on Wednesdays
with red tomato sauce.
    Fish and chips for Thursdays
    in a paper bag, of course.
Shepherd's pie for Fridays
with potatoes on the top.
    On Saturdays we have pizzas
    from Tony's Pizza Shop.
Sunday is a special day
  when we all sit down to tea
    for chicken roast and gravy,
      my dad, my mum, and me.

Moira Andrew

Ice-cream with Fish Fingers

Ice-cream with fish fingers,
Apple pie and greens.
Bread and butter pilchard pudding,
Custard and baked beans.

Marmite and bananas,
Biscuits dipped in stew.
All mixed up together
In an appetizing goo.

Strawberry milk shake, tea, and Coke,
And bits of bubble gum.
Just imagine what you'd see
Through a window in your tum.

Paul Bright

Where the Sausage Rolls

The sausage rolls in the ocean
the sausage rolls in the sea
the sausage rolls in the frying pan
then it rolls around in me.

Loris Lesynski

Cake-O-Saurus

Why don't we bake
a dinosaur cake
and call it Munchosaurus:

> Give it horns
> of ice-cream cones
> and call it Crunchosaurus.

Why don't we bake
a dinosaur cake
and call it Stickisaurus:

> Add gingernut eyes
> and buttercream thighs
> and call it Bickisaurus.

Why don't we bake
a dinosaur cake
and call it whatever we think:

> Then let it cool
> and eat it all
> until it is extinct.

Celia Warren

One Smiling Grandma

(A Caribbean Counting Rhyme)

One smiling grandma in a rocking chair,
Two yellow bows tied on braided hair.
Three humming birds sipping nectar sweet,
Four steel drums tapping out the beat,
Five flying fish gliding through the air,
Six market ladies selling their wares.
Seven conch shells I find on the beach,
Eight sugar apples, just out of reach.
Nine hairy coconuts, hard and round,
Ten sleepy mongoose. Hush! Not a sound.

Anne Marie Linden

Babies

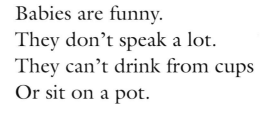

Babies are funny.
They don't speak a lot.
They can't drink from cups
Or sit on a pot.

They like to grip fingers.
They like milk from Mummies.
They like having raspberries
Blown on their tummies.

They like being cuddled
And kissed on the head.
But they don't say a lot,
They just dribble instead.

Michelle Magorian

Our New Baby

Sometimes I don't like our baby,
I don't like it when she yells.
I don't like it when she's all sniffly,
And I don't like it when she smells!

But mostly I do like our baby,
I like tickling her tiny pink feet,
And I like it best when she's on my knee
And I rock her until she's asleep.

Cynthia Rider

Leaky Baby

Our brand new baby's sprung a leak!
He's dripping like a spout,
We'd better send him back
Before his guarantee runs out.

Kaye Umansky

67

Dressing Up

When I dress up,
I always feel
just like a queen
in Mum's high heels.

I want to look
my queenly best,
so I'll put on
Mum's new long dress.

Crown jewels next.
Now let me see . . .
Where does Mum keep
her jewellery?

On royal lips
the queen then slicks
a nice thick layer
of Mum's lipstick.

Uh-uh! Here's Mum!
I fear the worst.
The queen forgot
to ask her first.

Jane Clarke

New Shoes

My shoes are new and squeaky shoes,
They're shiny, creaky shoes,
I wish I had my leaky shoes
That my mother threw away.

I liked my old brown leaky shoes
Much better than these creaky shoes,
These shiny, creaky, squeaky shoes,
I've got to wear today.

Anon.

Hard Work

Tying up laces is tiring—
Although I can make a good start—
I just get it right and then I pull tight,
But the bows that I tie fall apart.

Michelle Magorian

Tuesday's Tune

I'm playing a tune that I made up today,
And I'm banging the beat on my drum,
It goes trumpety crumpety squeakity squee,
Tiddle-tee-tiddle-toe-tiddle-tum.

The dog likes the tune that I made up today,
And we're singing it loudly for Mum,
Yaoowoo! Trumpety crumpety squeakity woof,
Tiddle-tee-tiddle-toe-tiddle-tum.

Petonelle Archer

70

Sorting Out the Kitchen Pans

We're sorting out the kitchen pans
   DING DONG BANG
Sorting out the kitchen pans
   BING BONG CLANG

Sorting out the kitchen pans
   TING BANG DONG
Sorting out the kitchen pans
   CLANG DING BONG

Sorting out the kitchen pans
   DONG DANG BONG
TING TANG BING BANG
   CLANG DING
       OW!

Quentin Blake

The Bubble Gum Competition

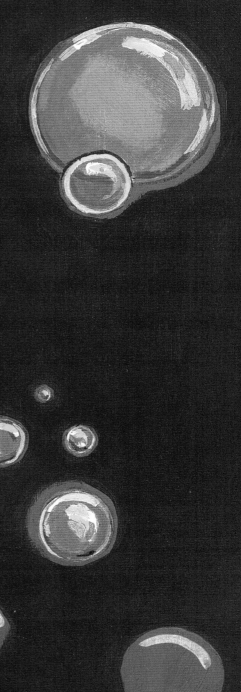

Billy blew a baby bubble,
Wanda blew one wider,
Babs breathed in instead of out—
Her bubble burst inside her.
'Right, watch me!' said Archie,
And he blew and blew and blew
And blew and blew a whopper,
And it grew and grew and grew
But grew too big, too powerful,
And you should have seen his face,
When the bubble lifted Archie
Off the earth and into space!

Richard Edwards

Who Shall I Be?

Today I'll be an astronaut
My mum says that's OK
But can I clear the mess up
Before I blast away?

Holly King

I Want . . .

I want to ride on a rainbow,
I want to swing on a star,
I want to cruise round a comet
And bring moonbeams home in a jar.

I want to be sprinkled with stardust,
I want to smile with the sun,
I want to play with the planets
Then zoom back through space when I'm done.

Clive Webster

Dance

Dance out of bed,
dance on the floor,
dance down the hallway,
dance out the door.

Dance in the morning,
dance in the night,
dance till the new moon
is out of sight.

Dance all summer,
autumn, and spring,
dance through the snowflakes
and don't forget to sing.

Eve Merriam

New Snow

The new new snow
is sparkling
in the sun.

Wherever I go
in the new new snow
I am
the
very
first one!

Lilian Moore

I'm a Freezy-Wheezy Snowman

I'm a freezy-wheezy snowman,
Will you warm me with a cuddle?
Oh, dear! I think I'm melting,
And now I'm . . . just . . . a . . . puddle.

Kaye Umansky

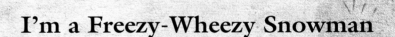

Reindeer

Far, far away
the reindeer live
in a land of ice
and snow . . .

When it's nearly
Christmas,
I wonder if
they know?

Nuzzling around
for a nibble of moss
in the freezing, arctic
day—

Do they guess
there's a sledge to pull
miles and miles
away?

Under a wide
star-sprinkled sky
that's shining
winter-bright,

Father Christmas
is loading up . . .
ready for
Christmas night!

Jean Kenward

Festivals and Parties

Festivals and parties
In the winter nights
Dressing up in party clothes
Pretty shiny lights.

Presents for our loved ones
Showing how we care
Eating lots of lovely food,
Remembering to share.

Festivals and parties
In the winter nights
Decorated houses
Making winter bright.

Brenda Williams

Sad

I'm sad in my tummy
And I don't know why
I don't feel like playing
I only want to cry.

I don't want a story
I don't want my tea
I just want to have a rest
On somebody's knee.

Michelle Magorian

Cuddle

I'd rather have a cuddle
than a video,
I'd rather have a cuddle
than anything I know,
I'd rather have a cuddle
than ketchup, chips, or peas,
a computer game is lovely
but—
a cuddle's what I need.

Peter Dixon

Squeezes

We love to squeeze bananas
We love to squeeze ripe plums
And when they are feeling sad
We love to squeeze our mums.

Brian Patten

Bath-time

In goes hot water,
Not too hot.
Squeeze out the bubble stuff,
In goes the lot.

In goes my whale
In goes my boat.
In go all the toys
That I can float.

Now my bath is ready
What else can there be?
I think I remember . . .
In goes ME.

Georgie Adams

Necks Time

I'm rather sorry for giraffes.
At bedtime when they take their baths
To wash their ears takes just two secs,
But it takes ten minutes to wash their necks!

David Whitehead

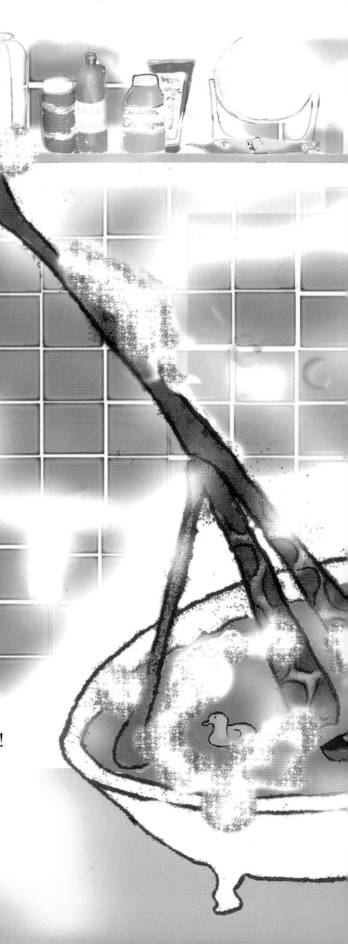

Into the Bathtub

Into the bathtub,
Great big splosh.
Toes in the bathtub,
Toes in the wash.

Soap's very slidy,
Soap smells sweet.
Soap all over,
Soap on your feet.

Rinse all the soap off,
Dirt floats away.
Dirt in the water.
Water's gone grey.

Out of the bathtub,
Glug, glug, glug.
Great big towel,
Great big hug.

Wendy Cope

The Hot-Air Monster

I hate the Hot-Air Monster,
I hate its boiling breath,
I hate the way it finds me,
I fight it to the death.

It comes out after bath-time,
it can't run very fast,
so I hide behind the sofa
to escape its fiery blast.

Mum finds me there and grabs me,
I twist between her knees,
she holds the Hot-Air Monster
and points its nose at me.

I yank up my pyjamas
to cover all my hair,
it noses down my armhole
and blows its fire in there.

Red hot scalding fury
burns my ears and head
but I battle with the monster
until it's time for bed.

I hate the Hot-Air Monster,
I hate its boiling breath,
I hate the way it finds me,
I fight it to the death.

Ellen Phethean

If You Were

If you were a sleepy,
Velvety mole,
You'd curl yourself up
In an underground hole.

If you were a wallaby
Baby, I vouch
You'd be tucked up at night
In your mother's warm pouch.

In the tropical forest
The young chimpanzees
Cling tight to their mums
Fast asleep in the trees.

If you slept like a tortoise
The whole winter through,
You'd miss all of Christmas
And New Year's Day, too.

So I think you'll agree,
From all I have said,
That the best place for YOU
Is your warm, comfy bed.

Barry On

Bedtime March-past

I need to cuddle Penguin.
I need to cuddle Sheep.
I need to cuddle Crocodile
before I go to sleep.

I need to cuddle Little Bear,
then tuck him out of sight,
before I kiss old Dinosaur
who sometimes likes to fight.

I need to cuddle Monster,
then hide beneath the heap.
Mum says I'm hard to find
when toys lie seven-deep.

I need to cuddle Cattypus
before I put out the light.
But last of all I kiss my mum
and *then* I say 'Goodnight.'

Moira Andrew

84

My Brother's Teddy

In bed, with my brother,
a teddy bear lies.
He's minus an arm.
He's lost one of his eyes.
His fur's worn away
his ears are askew
and he's torn here and there
where the dog's had a chew.
But my brother just loves him.
Get rid of him? Never!
He's going to keep him
for ever and ever.

Marian Swinger

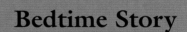

Bedtime Story

Dad's read my bedtime story
and down the stairs I creep.
I'm still very wide awake
but Dad is fast asleep.

Marian Swinger

Tooth Fairies

Daddy, Daddy,
tell me the truth.
What do the fairies
do with a tooth?

Well, my darling,
who can say
what takes place
beyond the day?

Perhaps they bury
those tiny bones
to carve them into
shining thrones.

Or take each white tooth
safely down
to cut themselves
a gleaming crown.

Perhaps they trim them
square and slick
to build a wall
that's sheer and thick.

Or take up neat
and nimble tools
to shape them into
necklace jewels.

For, dearest daughter,
who can say
what takes place
when we're away
or fast asleep
beyond the day?

Tony Mitton

All Night

Although it's night,
I think I might
Creep out of bed
And poke my head
Round Mummy's door—
Hear Daddy's snore!
And if I snuggle,
Diggle, duggle,
I think they may,
I think they might,
Let me stay
With them—all night!

Tony Bradman

87

Mummy, Daddy, Wake Up Quick!

Mummy, Daddy, wake up quick!
My tooth's gone wobbly! I'm feeling sick!
Mummy, Daddy, hey, you two!
Can I come and sleep with you?
Mummy, Daddy, wake up, please!
The window's open, I'm going to freeze!
Mummy, Daddy, no I'm not—
Take off the blanket, it's much too hot!
Mummy, Daddy, tell the truth,
Ever seen such a wobbly tooth?
Mummy, Daddy, what d'you think?
Should I go and get a drink?
Mummy, Daddy, please wake up,
I spilt my drink and broke the cup.
Mummy, Daddy, I've got an idea,
We could stay awake for the rest of the year!
Mummy, Daddy, what's that noise?
I heard a burglar stealing my toys.

Mummy, Daddy, open your eyes!
My tooth's come out—what a surprise!
Mummy, Daddy, I'm really unhappy,
I look so silly with my mouth all gappy.
Mummy, Daddy, wake up fast,
I think I'm going to sleep at last.
Mummy, Daddy, did you hear what I said?
You nearly pushed me off the bed!
Mummy, Daddy, put on the light!
Will the Tooth Fairy come tonight?
Mummy, Daddy, wake up soon!
Is there really a man in the moon?
Mummy, Daddy, one last thing,
When do the birds begin to sing?
Mummy, Daddy, don't try to hide,
Can't you see it's light outside?
Mummy, Daddy, stop that yawning!
You can't be tired, it's the middle of the morning!

Lawrence Anholt

Index of Titles and First Lines

(First lines are in italics)

Acknowledgements

We are grateful to the following for permission to include poems first published in this collection:

Tony Bradman: 'All Night', © Tony Bradman 2002, by permission of The Agency (London) Ltd. All rights reserved and enquiries to The Agency (London) Ltd, 24 Pottery Lane, London W11 4LZ; **Moira Andrew**: 'Food for the Week' and 'Bedtime March-past', © Moira Andrew 2002; **Petonelle Archer**: 'Tuesday's Tune', © Petonelle Archer 2002; **Clare Bevan**: 'Hide and Sheep', 'If I Were a Hawk', and 'The Beach Boys', © Clare Bevan 2002; **Paul Bright**: 'Ice-Cream With Fish Fingers', © Paul Bright 2002; **Alison Chisholm**: 'Going Swimming', © Alison Chisholm 2002; **Jane Clarke**: 'Sticky Syrup' and 'Dressing Up', © Jane Clarke 2002; **John Coldwell**: 'My Sister', © John Coldwell 2002; **Peter Dixon**: 'Waiting for Mum', © Peter Dixon 2002; **Richard Edwards**: 'The Bubble Gum Competition', © Richard Edwards 2002; **John Foster**: 'Jack the Yak', 'The Sandcastle', and 'See You Later, Escalator', © John Foster 2002; **Maureen Haselhurst**: 'Up on Daddy's Shoulders', © Maureen Haselhurst 2002; **Holly King**: 'Who Shall I Be?', © Holly King 2002; **John Kitching**: 'Knick Knack', © John Kitching 2002; **Wes Magee**: 'Here Come the Creatures', © Wes Magee 2002; **Trevor Millum**: 'Lively Lou and Lazy Lynn', © Trevor Millum 2002; **Judith Nicholls**: 'Ali's Dinner', © Judith Nicholls 2002; **Cynthia Rider**: 'Our New Baby' and 'My Roller Boots', © Cynthia Rider 2002; **Marian Swinger**: 'Marmaduke Monkey and Barnabas Bear', 'My Brother's Teddy', and 'Bedtime Story', © Marian Swinger 2002; **Clive Webster**: 'Best of All' and 'I Want …', © Clive Webster 2002; **David Whitehead**: 'Necks Time', © David Whitehead 2002; **Brenda Williams**: 'Katy Kelly' and 'Festivals and Parties', © Brenda Williams 2002.

We are also grateful for permission to include the following published poems:

Georgie Adams: 'Bath-time' from *A Year Full of Stories* (Orion Children's Books, 1997), reprinted by permission of the Orion Publishing Group Ltd; **John Agard**: 'Hopaloo Kangaroo' from *We Animals Would Like a Word With You* (Bodley Head, 1996), reprinted by permission of John Agard, c/o Caroline Sheldon Literary Agency; **Giles Andreae**: 'Octopus' from *Commotion in the Ocean* (first published in the UK by Orchard Books, 1998), reprinted by permission of the publishers, Orchard Books, a division of the Watts Publishing Group Ltd, and Tiger Tales, an imprint of ME Media LLC; **Laurence Anholt**: 'Mummy, Daddy, Wake Up Quick!' and 'Skirts and Shirts and Dressing Gowns' from *Catherine and Laurence Anholt's Big Book of Families* (1998), © Catherine & Laurence Anholt 1998, reprinted by permission of the publisher, Walker Books Ltd, London; **Quentin Blake**: 'Sorting Out the Kitchen Pans' from *All Join In* (Jonathan Cape, 1990), reprinted by permission of A. P. Watt Ltd on behalf of Quentin Blake; **James Carter**: 'There's Nothing' from *Electric Guitar* (Walker Books, 2002) reprinted by permission of the author; **Wendy Cope**: 'Into the Bathtub', © Wendy Cope 1999, reprinted by permission of the author; **June Crebbin**: 'The Dinosaur's Dinner' from *The Dinosaur's Dinner* (Viking, 1992), © June Crebbin 1992, reprinted by permission of the author; **John Cunliffe**: 'Humpty Dumpty' from *Incy Wincy Moo Cow* (Macdonald Young Books, 1999), reprinted by permission of David Higham Associates; **Peter Dixon**: 'Cuddle' from *The Colour of My Dreams* (Pan Macmillan, 2002), reprinted by permission of the author; **Malachy Doyle**: 'The Dancing Tiger', © Malachy Doyle 2000, first published in *Goodnight, Sleep Tight* compiled by Ivan and Mal Jones (Scholastic, 2000), reprinted by permission of the author; **Richard Edwards**: 'Yankee Doodle' and 'Up and Down the City Road' from *Nonsense Nursery Rhymes* (OUP, 1997), reprinted by permission of the author; **Anne English**: 'Summer Days' from *Poetry Corner* (Teacher's Notes), BBC Radio 1978, copyright holder not traced; **John Foster**: 'Rosemary Rudd', © John Foster 1999, from *Bare Bear* (OUP, 1999), reprinted by permission of the author; **Peggy Guthart**: 'Ready for Spaghetti' from *Poems for 5 Year Olds* (Macmillan), copyright holder not traced; **David Harmer**: 'Picnic Tea', © David Harmer 1999, first published in *Oxford Poetry Tree* compiled by John Foster (OUP, 1999), reprinted by permission of the author; **Jean Kenward**: 'Reindeer', © Jean Kenward 1999, first published in *Themes for Early Years* (Scholastic, 1999), reprinted by permission of the author; **Daphne Lister**: 'The Wuzzy Wasps of Wasperton', © Daphne Lister 1989, first published in *BBC Poetry Corner* (BBC, 1989); and 'Mumbling Bees', © Daphne Lister 1984, first published in *Sit on the Roof and Holler* compiled by Adrian Rumple (Puffin, 1984), reprinted by permission of the author; **Loris Lesynski**: 'Where the Sausage Rolls' from *Dirty Dog Boogie* (1999), reprinted by permission of the publisher, Annick Press Ltd; **Anne Marie Linden**: 'One Smiling Grandma' from *One Smiling Grandma: A Caribbean Counting Book* (Egmont Children's Books, 1996), text copyright © Anne Marie Linden 1992, reprinted by permission of the author and Egmont Books Ltd; **Ian McMillan**: 'The Dragon's Birthday Party' from *The Very Best of Ian McMillan* (Macmillan, 2001), reprinted by permission of the author; **Michelle Magorian**: 'Storm', 'Sad', and 'A Summer Afternoon' from *Waiting for my Shorts to Dry* (Viking, 1989); 'Babies' and 'Hard Work' from *Orange Paw Marks* (Puffin, 1991), copyright © Michelle Magorian 1989 and 1991, reprinted by permission of the author c/o Rogers, Coleridge & White Ltd, 20 Powis Mews, London W11 1JN; **Eve Merriam**: 'Weather' from *Jamboree Rhymes For All Times* (Dell, 1962), © 1962, 1964, 1966, 1973, 1984 Eve Merriam; 'Gooseberry Juiceberry' from *Blackberry Ink* (Morrow Jr, 1985) © 1985 Eve Merriam; and 'Dance' from *Higgle, Wiggle* (Morrow Jr, 1994) © 1994 The Estate of Eve Merriam; all reprinted by permission of Marian Reiner; **Tony Mitton**: 'Tooth Fairies' from *Pip* (Scholastic, 2001), © Tony Mitton 2001, reprinted by permission of the author; **Lilian Moore**: 'Hey, Bug!' from *I Feel the Same Way*, © 1967, 1995 Lilian Moore, reprinted by permission of Marian Reiner for the author; 'Finger Paints' and 'New Snow' from *I'm Small and Other Verses* (2001), © 2001 Lilian Moore, reprinted by permission of the publishers Walker Books Ltd, London; **Aislinn and Larry O'Loughlin**: 'Our Dog' from *Worms Can't Fly* (Wolfhound Press, 2000), © Aislinn and Larry O'Loughlin, reprinted by permission of Merlin Publishing; **Barry On**: 'If You Were' from *Goodnight, Sleep Tight* compiled by Ivan and Mal Jones (Scholastic Press, 2000), copyright © Barry On 2000, reprinted by permission of the author c/o Rogers, Coleridge & White Ltd, 20 Powis Mews, London W11 1JN; **Brian Patten**: 'Squeezes' from *Gargling with Jelly* (Viking, 1985), © Brian Patten 1985, reprinted by permission of Penguin Books Ltd and the author c/o Rogers, Coleridge & White Ltd, 20 Powis Mews, London W11 1JN; **Ellen Phethean**: 'The Hot-Air Monster', © Ellen Phethean 1998, first published in *Shimmy with my Granny* chosen by Sarah Garland (Macdonald Young Books, 1998), reprinted by permission of the author; **Jack Prelutsky**: 'Jilliky Jolliky Jelliky Jee' from *Ride a Purple Pelican* (Greenwillow Books, 1986), text © Jack Prelutsky 1986, reprinted by permission of HarperCollins Publishers; **Michael Rosen**: 'Mary Anne' from *Michael Rosen's Book of Nonsense* (Macdonald Young Books, 1997), © Michael Rosen 1997, reprinted by permission of PFD on behalf of Michael Rosen; **Mollie Russell-Smith**: 'Wide Awake' retitled 'When All the Cows were Sleeping' from *Wide Awake* (Mills Music Ltd), words by Mollie Russell-Smith, music by Geoffrey Russell-Smith, © EMI Mills Music Inc., USA. Worldwide print rights controlled by Warner Bros Publications Inc./IMP Ltd, reprinted by permission of International Music Publications Ltd. All rights reserved; **Gordon Snell**: 'The Hamster's Wheel' from *The Thursday Club* (Dolphin, 2000, Orion Children's Books), reprinted by permission of the Orion Publishing Group Ltd; **Kaye Umansky**: 'Leaky Baby', first published in *Shimmy with my Granny* chosen by Sarah Garland (Macdonald Young Books, 1998); and 'I'm a Freezy-Wheezy Snowman', first published in *Tickle My Nose* (Puffin, 1999), reprinted by permission of the author; 'One Man Went to Mow' from *Nonsense Counting Rhymes* (OUP, 1999), and 'Gorilla!' and 'Bored!' from *Nonsense Animal Rhymes* (OUP, 2001), reprinted by permission of Kaye Umansky, c/o Caroline Sheldon Literary Agency; **Gregor Vitez**: 'Catch Me the Moon, Daddy' from *Catch Me the Moon, Daddy* compiled by Walter Kaufman (1997), reprinted by permission of the publishers, Kingscourt/McGraw Hill; **Celia Warren**: 'Cake-O-Saurus', © Celia Warren 1994, first published in *Got You, Pirate!* compiled by John Foster (OUP, 1994), reprinted by permission of the author; **Colin West**: 'Rolling Down a Hill' from *What Would You Do With a Wobble-Dee-Woo?* (Hutchinson, 1988), reprinted by permission of the author; **Jeanne Willis**: 'Zanzibar' from *Toffee Pockets* (Bodley Head, 1992), reprinted by permission of The Random House Group Ltd.

Despite every effort to trace and contact copyright holders before publication this has not been possible in every case. If notified, the publisher will be pleased to rectify any errors or omissions at the earliest opportunity.

Index of Artists

All the artists commissioned for this book are graduates, with the exception of Kristin Oftedal who is a first year student, and Tony Ross who isn't.

Catch Me the Moon, Daddy

Catch me the moon, Daddy,
Let it shine near me for a while,
Catch me the moon, Daddy,
I want to touch its smile.

The moon must shine from high above;
That's where it needs to stay
Among the stars, to guide them home
When they return from play.

So the bunny can find his supper,
So the mouse can scamper free,
So the hedgehog can make his forays,
So the birds can sleep in the tree.

And as for you, my child,
With slender silver thread
The moon will weave sweet dreams, so you
May slumber in your bed.

Gregor Vitez